100 AWESOME IDEAS FOR AUTHORS

Have Fun With Your Writing and Sell More Books

COURTNEY KENNEY

COPYRIGHT

© **2017 Courtney Kenney. All rights reserved.**
ISBN-13: 978-1974140947

CONTENTS

Introduction	vii
How to Use This Book	1

Part 1
PART ONE: WRITING AND CREATIVITY

1. Become a Story Junkie	5
2. Reinvent History	6
3. Look Ma, No Pants	7
4. When Selling Out is Not a Bad Thing	8
5. Make Your Book Stink	9
6. Jump Start Your Writing Productivity	10
7. What If You Were an Alien?	11
8. Just 100 Words	12
9. Storyboard Your Book with Pinterest	13
10. Write the Story Within the Story	14
11. Let Music Be Your Muse	15
12. How to Know Your Genre	16
13. Get Lectured	17
14. Robots Gone Wild	18
15. Invent a New Word	19
16. Be Efficient with the Space in Each Scene	20
17. Build a World Where You Are the Boss	21
18. Date Your Inner Artist	23
19. Got TED?	24
20. The ABCs of Writing	25

Part 2
PART TWO: EDITING AND POLISHING YOUR BOOK

21. Get Over Yourself...	29
22. Exile Perfection	31
23. Draw a Map	32

24. Lights, Camera, Action!	33
25. The Three Questions You Must Ask Yourself	34
26. Put Editing on Autopilot	35
27. Jedi Mind Tricks for Better, Faster Editing	36
28. Banish These Words	38
29. Show Me the Money	39
30. What Would Hemingway Do?	40
31. I'll Show You Mine...	41
32. Toss Your Outline	42
33. Train Your Brain for Editing	43
34. One Scene at a Time	44
35. Create Space in Each Scene	45
36. My Dog Ate My Novel!	46
37. Begin with the End	47
38. Two Wise Guys	48
39. Device Hop	49
40. Be Loud	50

Part 3
PART THREE: ENGAGING WITH READERS AND CREATING TRUE FANS

41. Survey Says...	53
42. Hang Out	54
43. Say Thanks	55
44. How to Handle Lousy Reviews	56
45. Co-Write with Other Authors	57
46. Be an Exhibitionist	58
47. The Library Is Your Friend	59
48. Don't Forget Indie Bookstores	60
49. It's All Who You Know	62
50. Reign in Your Social Media	64
51. Create a Quick and Easy Email Course	66
52. Let Your Writing Shine on Wattpad	67
53. When Fiction Becomes (Augmented) Reality	68
54. What Would Only a Native Know?	69
55. Listen to the Experts	70
56. Grow Your Reader List Faster Than a Chia Pet	71
57. Title This!	73
58. The Secret of My Success	74

59. Yes, and...	75
60. Persuasion Principles	76

Part 4
PART FOUR: MARKETING TO SELL MORE BOOKS

61. The Breakfast Club	81
62. Lessons Learned—Own It!	82
63. Gimme, Gimme Some Giveaways	83
64. The Pulp Fiction Secret	84
65. The Holy Grail of Book Advertising	86
66. Merchandise Your Book	88
67. If You Build It, They Will Come	89
68. Embrace Artificial Intelligence	90
69. The Golden Age of Television	91
70. Market Like a Pro	93
71. Creating Content at an Elite Level	95
72. Earn Income While You Sleep	96
73. Where the Buyers Are – Amazon Ads	97
74. Spy on Your Readers	99
75. Dear Diary	101
76. Winning. Everyone Loves a Contest	102
77. Go Wide	104
78. Get Out of the Writer's Cave	106
79. If We Took A Holiday...	108
80. Podcast-a-palooza	109

Part 5
PART FIVE: POSITIVE MINDSET AND TAKING CARE OF YOURSELF

81. Just Say No	113
82. The Wall of Shame	114
83. Go on a Writer's Retreat	115
84. Ditch Negative Self-Talk	116
85. Be the Rising Tide	117
86. Throw a Book Funeral	118
87. Take a Ridiculous Writer's Vacation	119
88. The Wondrous World of Ideas Around You	120
89. Trust Emergence	122
90. Repeat After Me...	123

91. Health Hacks for Your Writer's Bod	125
92. What Is Success?	126
93. Meet Future You	128
94. Toot That Horn	129
95. Build a Treadmill Desk	130
96. Ride in the Back of a Police Car	131
97. Abandon Your Guilt	132
98. Give Back	133
99. Soak in the Suds	134
100. Get Your Mojo Back	135
Conclusion	137
About the Author	139

INTRODUCTION

Sometimes as writers we take ourselves too seriously! We can forget to have fun when we get caught up in writing, editing, and marketing our books in what may sometimes feel like an endless loop.

Do you know the feeling?

There are moments when we want to bang our heads against the desk, when we get stuck in the saggy middles of our stories.

Sometimes we pour our hearts into a novel and don't see the sales results that we deserve. Nevertheless, we dust ourselves off and start writing the next book.

Content is gold. Remember that your story is valuable, and it's your job as a writer to create, inspire, and entertain the world.

This book is a reminder that this writing life is supposed to be, above all, fun!

Have you ever thought about finding the humor in your daily challenges? How about adding a little wackiness to your writing life?

This is a different to-do list than what you may normally

use. Instead, here are 100 ideas that will help you the next time you are stuck.

In these pages, discover how to:

- Overcome writer's block and get inspired again.
- Escape the doldrums of editing—change your mindset, find tools that will save you time, and more.
- Engage with your readers, grow your email list, and create **true** fans who will want to read everything you write.
- Market your book in unique and exciting ways. Sell more books while avoiding overwhelm and shiny object syndrome.
- Take care of your body and mind with mindset tricks, health hacks, and more.

I hope you'll enjoy it, and find a few ideas that may help the next time you're stuck not knowing what to write, or find yourself agonizing over a plot twist.

HOW TO USE THIS BOOK

This book is organized into five key areas that make up the writer's life:

- Writing and Creativity
- Editing and Polishing Your Book
- Engaging with Readers and Creating True Fans
- Marketing to Sell More Books
- Positive Mindset and Taking Care of Yourself

This book isn't meant to be read page by page, although you're certainly welcome to do so. Keep the book handy so that when you're stuck in an area such as editing, you can flip to that chapter and read a few ideas.

Do you take vitamins? Think of this book as 100 two-minute digestible writer vitamins!

Some of the ideas may not be entirely new to you, but my hope is that they will serve as good reminders.

Other ideas are unconventional, even strange. I hope you get some laughs from this book and can use some of the ideas in real life.

As you read, you may come up with things you would have included. Email your ideas to info@projectmanagerwriter.com, and I may include them with your name in a future edition.

Happy Writing,
Courtney Kenney
ProjectManagerWriter.com

PART ONE: WRITING AND CREATIVITY

1
BECOME A STORY JUNKIE

I'm always amazed at the stories that surround us.

Living in a big city, I take a lot of taxi rides and hear the most interesting stories from the drivers. Always remember that the people in our lives that we may not think about—the package delivery guy, the grocery checkout clerk, our Uber driver—all have interesting stories, *if* we take the time to listen to them.

Be sure to carry a small notebook to capture observations. When possible, listen and engage with new people. Consider carrying a business card—you never know what interesting connections you'll make. I met a Lyft driver who was a freelance sound editor and turned out to be a great connection for finding a studio for audiobook recording.

2

REINVENT HISTORY

Can you twist history?

For example, if my character lived in ancient Rome, he could have changed the way they_____?

Or you could reinvent an old classic. Why is the *Sherlock* TV show starring Benedict Cumberbatch so entertaining? The writers have retold the same story of Sherlock and Dr. Watson, but added a modern twist, even turning Watson into a blogger.

Consider the book (now a television show), *The Man in The High Castle*. Philip K. Dick asked a compelling question: What if the Germans and Japanese had won World War II? In doing so, a whole new world can be imagined.

In what interesting and unique ways can you reshape history? Do this well, and your story will write itself.

3
LOOK MA, NO PANTS

What is your preferred writing style? Are you a plotter or a pantser?

Plotters write to an outline that is carefully developed, whereas pantsers are flying by the seat of their pants, letting the plot develop as they write.

Most of us are probably somewhere in the middle. Many writers I know, me included, develop an outline, but sometimes our scenes go in different directions when we get caught up in writing.

Have you ever tried writing a short story or novella without pants? Try taking an idea and writing scene by scene, without an outline. You might not end up liking the end result, but at least you'll have tried something new.

4
WHEN SELLING OUT IS NOT A BAD THING

We should write what we love, but have you ever thought about writing a book to market? Author Chris Fox wrote a book called *Write to Market*. He includes exercises about how to research books in a specific genre, and how to find a "hungry" genre—one in which the readers are under-served and eager to read new content.

It's worth trying at least once as an author. Fox advocates finding the required tropes within a genre. For example, space military fiction books should have a giant starship on the cover and be about a ragtag crew with a maverick captain who is humanity's last hope against an evil force.

Does that sound constraining? While writing within limits is required, you can still put your unique spin on the content and make it your own.

Fox argues that you can make more income as an author by applying his principles. Hey, it's worth trying out, right?

5
MAKE YOUR BOOK STINK

Ever wondered to yourself, "How does this scene smell?" If your scene (or your story) stinks, then you may have a problem!

But seriously, consider using your five senses when writing. During a conversation between characters, what are you hearing and not hearing? Are those sirens in the distance or cries for help?

What does your main character want so badly that she can taste it? Your villain?

Describe the sensations the character feels when touching an object.

Also, what do the characters see that can be mentioned in dialog rather than written as a description?

6

JUMP START YOUR WRITING PRODUCTIVITY

Scrivener is a writing tool available from LiteratureAndLatte.com. There's a free trial, and the software sells for around $40 USD. It's a bargain. The tool has changed the lives of many writers, including me.

How? You can create a Scrivener project for each of your books. Then, write each scene or chapter, and easily drag and drop chapters if you need to revise your structure. It's amazing and allows your story to be fluid and flexible.

Use Scrivener to compile your book into several formats: Microsoft Word, PDF, Mobi file for Kindle, and ePUB.

Do you write blogs? Write them as separate chapters inside a Scrivener project. You'll have your articles in one place rather than having to search through computer files. And if you ever lose your website and didn't back it up, you'll be able to retrieve your content.

❼
WHAT IF YOU WERE AN ALIEN?

Pretend you are an alien sent from a remote planet. You've just arrived on earth on a mission to observe and report back on the inhabitants.

Take a trip into the nearest big city. Pretend you are an alien tourist. What would you think of this world? Jot down ideas into a notebook or on your phone.

Next, consider what trouble you can get into. What if you —alien tourist—are enjoying planet Earth but are suddenly instructed by your home planet to destroy it? What if you fell in love with an earthling? This is sounding more and more complicated—and fascinating!

8
JUST 100 WORDS

Some days it can be so hard to write. We all feel this way from time to time. We get that dreaded feeling of staring at a blank screen and not feeling like we have any good ideas. At times, we feel tapped out or creatively empty.

On days like these, it's hard to push through and keep writing. Think 100 words at a time. It should take just a few minutes to write 100 words. Then string together another 100 words.

Get enough 100-word chunks written, and you'll soon reach 1,000 words or more.

This mindset works well for those of us who don't always write in order from beginning to end.

9

STORYBOARD YOUR BOOK WITH PINTEREST

Pinterest.com has an incredible variety of photos, artwork, and just about anything you can think of. Create a board for your new book and pin photos that you find on Pinterest and other websites.

Let's say you're writing a novel about circus life. Search "circus" on Pinterest, and you'll be amazed at the images you find. Pin them to the new board you have created, and use this as inspiration for your writing.

The best part? You can later share your Pinterest board with your readers for a behind-the-scenes glimpse into your writing world.

10

WRITE THE STORY WITHIN THE STORY

We all know that stories have three parts: a beginning, a middle, and an end. Your novel should follow that structure, and so should a blog, short story, or non-fiction book.

But have you gone deeper? Think of **each chapter** as its own story, with a beginning, middle, and end. Editor/author Shawn Coyne talks about this in the StoryGrid podcast. Using this simple structure can help you get through plot challenges as you're writing.

Think about each chapter as a story within your overarching story. What is happening to your character? Say your chapter starts with "Jeff goes to the store." What does he say or do on his way there? What is he seeking?

Then, what happens next at the store? Does he run into his neighbor or an archenemy? Describe their encounter. What mood are you trying to convey? Then, finally, how does the scene end? Does Jeff throw eggs at his rival and get kicked out of the store? Will a cleanup in aisle four be necessary?

When you start to consider each scene/chapter this way, writing gets easier.

11
LET MUSIC BE YOUR MUSE

Studies show music can help us be more creative. A 2011 Finnish study demonstrated that music activates our brain toward creative thought.

Music is also a great pick-me-up when you're feeling down, and streaming stations like Pandora and Spotify make it easy to create custom playlists.

Many authors create playlists for a specific book and use that to inspire their writing. Consider setting up a playlist that your main character or the villain would love.

Author Joanna Penn listens to sounds of thunder and rain when she writes in cafes. Stephanie Meyers, author of the *Twilight* series, listened to Muse when she wrote her books.

I enjoy listening to streaming radio, which lets you choose a band, then the software chooses songs by similar artists. Check out the Echo and the Bunnymen channel for some inspiring 1980s tunes.

12
HOW TO KNOW YOUR GENRE

Successful authors have something in common: They read a lot. The best writers know their genres inside and out. They keep up with the hot new releases and keep a finger on the bestseller lists in the categories in which they write.

If you're writing for the long term, and want this to be your career, then you need to treat it as such. Consider that doctors, lawyers, and accountants must keep up with the latest trends and news in their industries. So should writers.

Dedicate a set time each week to sit down and browse the bestseller lists on Amazon. Check out the specials on Bookbub.com. Look at the *New York Times* and *USA Today* bestseller lists. What are readers buying? The more you do this, the more it will become like second nature.

Before you start to write in a new genre, be sure to read at least three of the top sellers in that niche. Note what is similar and different about each story. What are the readers saying in the five-star reviews (and, more importantly, in the one-star reviews)? What do you notice about the covers of each book? These are the key ingredients you want to mimic to try and break into the bestseller list in a category.

13
GET LECTURED

Attend a lecture on a topic that sounds interesting, and is new to you. Many universities and museums offer lectures. Maybe you will enjoy a topic like neuropsychology or entomology.

You might learn something and be inspired to use that subject in your story. What if you learn something cool about butterflies and decide to make your main character an entomologist?

After the class, read one or two books by specialists in that field so you get an understanding of the field of study and day-to-day life.

14
ROBOTS GONE WILD

Artificial Intelligence (AI) is certain to factor into our future work and everyday lives.

Personally, I'm excited about the rise of AI personal assistants. Google Assistant allows us to find help and automate online research. Amazon Echo has been a top-selling new technology device since 2016. Apple and Google are stepping up with similar products.

Write about what would happen if you received an AI personal assistant as a gift and things went horribly wrong. What if your robot VA stole from you or tried to assume your identity?

15
INVENT A NEW WORD

What if you could create a new word that would make it into the genre in which you write? How fun would that be?

J.R.R. Tolkien invented new languages, and words like "hobbit" and "orc" have influenced generations of writers.

While achieving Tolkienesque heights may not be realistic for 99% of us, can you add something to your genre for which others will remember you?

Consider it a challenge and have fun.

16

BE EFFICIENT WITH THE SPACE IN EACH SCENE

I attended a talk given by phenomenal author Veronica Roth, of *Divergent* fame. Something she said stood out: "I try to be efficient with the space in each scene." She explained that she tries to make each scene accomplish many things at once.

When you're writing a scene, what is your main goal, and what else can you add?

Let's say you have a scene where a girl has gone missing, and a detective arrives at the family home to question the family. Your primary goal might be to advance the story, but what else can you show? How does the little sister react? Is the father present? Other family members? Does something seem odd or out of place about the living room? What subliminal clues can you introduce that may later influence your plot?

17

BUILD A WORLD WHERE YOU ARE THE BOSS

The concept of world-building can be intimidating for writers of fantasy or science-fiction. I know it scares me to think about it.

Try making it more fun by appointing yourself CWB (chief world builder). You are completely in charge. Everyone in your world must bow to you and kiss your feet.

Now, have some fun. What rules would you have in your world? Would you want everything to be perfect, or a little mischievous?

What laws of science or nature can you break? For example, in the book, *The Leftovers*, author Tom Perrotta chronicled an event in which 2% of the world's population abruptly disappears without explanation. This violates the laws of nature as we know them, but it works in his imaginary world. The mystery is so great, it leaves readers wanting to find out what happened.

Ask yourself what is unique about your world. Maybe some people can fly but others can't. Why? And what happens when someone discovers how to fly even though they shouldn't? These are the types of hooks that will leave readers wanting more.

18
DATE YOUR INNER ARTIST

Julia Cameron writes about artist dates in her book, *The Artist's Way: A Spiritual Path to Higher Creativity*. An artist date is an appointment where you fill your creative well. Find an activity or a place that inspires you. For some, this might be a park on a beautiful day with a notebook and pen. For others, a museum may provide inspiration.

The point is to be open-minded and present on your artist date. Capture your thoughts, observations, and experiences. The more you take the time to replenish yourself as an artist, the better it will be for your creativity.

Start small and set aside one afternoon per month for your date. Experiment and try new experiences that are not as comfortable.

19
GOT TED?

There are a ridiculous number of inspiring lectures on TED.com, on every topic imaginable. Browse their home page and find a talk on a subject about which you know nothing.

Listen to a different talk every day for a week. At the end of your week, choose a talk and use the subject in a new story.

What if an entomologist gave the talk? Perhaps your new main character spent years studying the mating habits of fireflies. Wouldn't that make for an interesting back story? How does the firefly research impact his or her own relationships?

20

THE ABCS OF WRITING

Always
   Be
      Creating

Did you ever see the movie *Glengarry Glen Ross* with Alec Baldwin, where he delivers his "Always be closing" lecture?

There's also a hilarious holiday *Saturday Night Live* sketch where Baldwin gives the same speech, only he's Santa talking to elves, and the mantra is "Always be cobbling."

As writers, we owe it to ourselves to **always be creating**—writing and creating assets that will be your next book or reader magnet, or honing your next marketing tactic.

Indie writers don't have a big publishing company behind them to sell for them. As authors in the digital age, we must go beyond traditional marketing tactics and leverage content marketing, SEO, and social media. All of this can get overwhelming. Trust me, I know.

One thing remains constant: Writers write. So, always be creating.

PART TWO: EDITING AND POLISHING YOUR BOOK

21
GET OVER YOURSELF...

Your negative mindset, that is.

After you've spent hours upon hours writing your first draft, and finally reached your target word count, it's time to celebrate, right? Yes, of course. You've achieved a great milestone.

But remember the next part—the editing phase.

Editing sucks. There, I said it. For many writers, it's the worst part of finishing a book. Some of us, me included, will spend years editing our first novel.

For others, editing comes easy (I'm jealous).

Why must we edit our own work? Can't we just ship off our manuscripts to an editor and let him or her work it out? Unfortunately, one of the biggest mistakes new writers make is skipping the self-edit. In other words, never send an unedited first draft to an editor or agent. The editing process starts with the writer self-editing.

What's the real purpose of editing? When you edit, you turn a pile of words into an amazing story that will inspire, delight, and entertain your readers. Editing is where you put yourself into the reader's head. What parts of your manuscript will keep readers turning pages and seeking answers? What parts will bore them?

That's the real skill with editing. Change your mindset away from dreading the editing process. Instead, realize you are polishing your manuscript so that the real story can shine through.

22
EXILE PERFECTION

Editing can go on for years if we let it. But, we don't have time for that, do we? You need to get on with editing your book so you can move on to the next one.

Consider the Pareto 80/20 principle. According to this principle, 80% of our results come from 20% of our efforts. This rule is repeated across nature and economies.

What is the 20% of your book that is most important? Certainly, story structure and theme is important. You can have a well-written book, but if the story doesn't hook a reader, you will disappoint.

At some point, too much editing yields diminishing returns. Letting go of perfection and releasing your book into the world is the best way to move ahead. Concentrate on producing the best story experience you can; readers will forgive a few typos for an excellent tale.

23
DRAW A MAP

An editing tip I picked up from author Rachel Aaron is to build a scene map of your book. In this process, you page through your manuscript and write down what happens in each chapter. Often, what you actually wrote may differ from your original outline. A scene map helps you later on when you need to go back and rewrite.

A scene map also helps you identify problem areas. Where does your action drop off? Is a chapter boring? If it's boring to you, imagine how it will feel to a reader.

24

LIGHTS, CAMERA, ACTION!

Skim through your book and play a movie reel in your head. This works well when you have a scene map that helps you visualize your book as a movie.

What parts can you imagine easily? Those are likely the best parts of your story. The parts that feel weird, or that you struggle to envision, are the parts you need to go back and reconsider.

Also, think of your favorite movies for inspiration. Struggling with your opening scene? Go back and look at movies with great opening scenes, like *Raiders of the Lost Ark*, *Star Wars IV: A New Hope*, and *Pulp Fiction*. What is it that made those movies pull you into their stories?

How do you want your movie to play out?

THE THREE QUESTIONS YOU MUST ASK YOURSELF

Read your book and ask yourself the following three questions for each chapter:

1. What is the point of this chapter?
2. What new information does the reader learn?
3. How does this chapter move the story forward?

Each chapter should serve a purpose. Asking these questions helps you identify chapters that may not add value and should be cut. Don't delete. Hold onto your discarded chapters in case you want to use them for something else later (e.g., a free back-story download on your website).

26
PUT EDITING ON AUTOPILOT

Make life easier by purchasing an editing software tool such as Grammarly. Not only will using an editing tool help you catch typos and grammar mistakes, it also helps you with sentence structure and tells you where you have overused words.

I recommend going premium to get the advanced features. Keep in mind the software shouldn't replace a professional editor, but it greatly reduces the time you spend on your self-edits.

Grammarly also works well when writing blogs and emails.

JEDI MIND TRICKS FOR BETTER, FASTER EDITING

You may be thinking: "Editing still sucks!" You have a point. Here are a few other mind tricks to get through the editing process:

- Track your time spent editing and make it a challenge to get faster.
- Realize that all writers go through the editing process. We share your pain!
- Focus on one small piece at a time. When you think about editing an entire manuscript at once, it's overwhelming. Instead, have a checklist that you use every time you edit a book. Step one is mapping the story structure, step two is editing your intro, step three is fixing the ending, and so on.
- Focus on structure, plot, and theme at first. Later, work on word choice and line edits.
- Use software (e.g., Grammarly). Automation is your friend.

- Use your computer's built-in text-to-voice feature to listen to your manuscript.

BANISH THESE WORDS

There are words that writers tend to overuse. The good news is that you can search for and eliminate those words. Here's a list of words you probably don't need:

- Look for "up" and "down."
- "That" - use only for clarity
- Check for adjectives. Use sparingly.
- Avoid hedging words ("slightly," "almost," "a bit").
- Avoid the term "literally."

29
SHOW ME THE MONEY

One of the hardest things for new writers is the concept of "show, don't tell." We all know about it, and we try to adhere, but it's tough, especially when we're writing the first draft. This is why editing is so important. If we do our editing job well, we'll go back and rework our drafts to make sure we're showing.

Lucy was about to lose her mind with jealousy. Furious, she threw her glass into the fireplace and demanded, "It's me or the robot!"

Instead, write:

Lucy threw her glass into the fireplace and locked eyes on Jordan. "Marry me and lose the robot."

Likewise, avoid telling what's not happening. Don't write, "He didn't reply" or "The sirens never stopped wailing." If you don't say these things happened, then the reader will assume they didn't.

30

WHAT WOULD HEMINGWAY DO?

Ernest Hemingway (1899-1961) was known for his bold, clear writing style. His spare, tight prose made Hemingway famous and influenced generations of writers. He won the Nobel prize in 1954 for "mastery of the art of narrative."

My secret weapon for checking my writing is clear is a website called hemingwayapp.com. Paste in your text and the software will flag any sentences that are hard to read. It identifies adverbs you can discard, indicates where to turn passive voice into active, and provides simpler word choices.

Try it out. It's free and awesome.

31
I'LL SHOW YOU MINE...

Do you utterly despise editing? Are you out there? I feel your pain.

When all else fails, maybe you give up editing entirely.

Do you know another author who thinks editing sucks as much as you do? Consider the idea of an editing swap, where you exchange drafts with each other. Often, it's easier to edit someone else's work than to face your own. The exercise of an editing swap may even give you the emotional distance you need to come back to your manuscript and prepare it for publishing.

32

TOSS YOUR OUTLINE

Ever finished a first draft manuscript and felt it was mediocre or that something was missing?

After you've finished writing your book, write a new outline by changing certain events. What if the character made a different decision? How would that affect the story?

Don't let this process stress you out. Just consider an alternate outline with an open mind. There are no good or bad outlines, just better ones.

You may end up discarding your alternate outline, but perhaps this technique will give you a surprising new plot twist that will keep your readers guessing.

33

TRAIN YOUR BRAIN FOR EDITING

Productive writers track their daily word count. It's important to write and work our creative muscles.

Have you ever thought about tracking the time you spend editing? Editing is just as important as writing, and it uses different parts of your brain. I heard the idea of tracking your editing progress from indie author Bryan Cohen.

Cohen suggests the fastest way to write the first draft is to write without editing. Don't think about your sentence structure, word choice, or anything involving editing. Otherwise, you will be much slower to finish, or may never finish at all!

He recommends writers devote a chunk of their day to editing and tracking their progress.

I've often put off the hard work of editing because it's not as fun as writing the first draft. If you struggle with editing too, consider tracking time spent or the number of words edited.

Whether you're editing a book or a blog post, track the time. Just like writing, the more you do it, the easier it will become.

34
ONE SCENE AT A TIME

In her book *Bird by Bird*, Anne Lamott tells a story about her brother being incredibly stressed out as a boy because he had a project to write about 30 birds, and had procrastinated until the night before. She captures a beautiful moment where her father patiently sat down with her anxious brother and said, "Ok. Let's work on this. We'll go bird by bird."

I always think about that story whenever I'm feeling overwhelmed. I step back and ask myself, "What can I work on right now that will move me forward?" Usually, there's an answer, and I start working on it.

Think about editing a manuscript in the same way. Instead of focusing on how much work is required to edit 80,000 words, go scene by scene.

When you use a software tool such as Scrivener, this becomes even easier because you can move from scene to scene, and drag and drop if you need to rearrange sections.

35

CREATE SPACE IN EACH SCENE

Creating space for creativity is something I think about a lot. I was fortunate to attend an event where I heard Veronica Roth (author of the phenomenal *Divergent* series) speak.

Something Veronica said stood out. She writes her books one scene at a time. The project manager in me loves this concept of breaking things down into smaller parts.

Then, Veronica said, "I try to be efficient with the space in each scene," explaining that she tries to make each scene accomplish many things at once.

Her idea resonated with me. As you edit, consider the space in each scene. What is your character achieving? Can something else be revealed within that scene? What new event can occur that will keep your reader turning the page?

36

MY DOG ATE MY NOVEL!

Back up your work. I include this because I know how painful it is to lose work when your computer crashes. Once, I spent hours editing, didn't save my work, and then lost it to a computer reboot.

Not fun.

How do you back up your writing projects? Like everything, backups take time. Consider an automated tool such as Carbonite that works in the background to save your work to the cloud every night.

It's also a good idea to keep a Google Drive (or other cloud application) where you save the latest version of your books in case you ever have a complete hard drive melt down.

Spending a little time to set up a backup system could save you a lot of heartache down the road.

37
BEGIN WITH THE END

Have you ever read a book that was well written and kept you turning the pages, but then disappointed you at the end? That's happened to me many times. An ending that doesn't satisfy your readers causes negative word of mouth, and readers will skip your new books.

Spend time polishing and revising your ending to make it the best it can be for your readers. Grill your beta readers on the ending. What did they think? Ask why, and don't just take superficial answers.

38
TWO WISE GUYS

I had a professor in college who required his students to buy *The Elements of Style* by William Strunk Jr. and E.B. White. This book was originally published in 1920 and has stood the test of time.

One of the most important instructions from the book is "Omit needless words."

Dorothy Parker once said, "If you have any young friends who aspire to become writers, the second-greatest favor you can do them is to present them with copies of *The Elements of Style*. The first-greatest, of course, is to shoot them now, while they're happy."

Thank you, Professor Jacobs, for introducing this book to thousands of students. I often refer to my yellowing, frayed copy when I'm editing.

39
DEVICE HOP

When you write a full-length manuscript in Scrivener, Microsoft Word, Google Docs, or your tool of choice, you become accustomed to reading your work in that environment.

As you start to edit, I encourage you to try and mix up how you're reading your manuscript. For example, print your work and read on paper.

Or, try loading your work-in-progress to a device such as a tablet or a Kindle. This allows you to read as if you were someone buying the book online.

It's also pretty thrilling to see your work of art on a device.

40
BE LOUD

As we write, we type out the monologue in our heads as fast as we can. We think and speak faster than we write, so our thoughts often get ahead of the words we are getting down on paper.

Your first draft should be written as fast as possible, without self-censoring. When you go back to re-read for the first time, try reading your work out loud. You may catch awkward phrases. Sometimes we "hear" typos or grammatical errors more frequently than our eyes can catch them.

As you read out loud, think about how your book would sound if it were an audio book. Imagine a reader hearing your audio book. This simple trick—reading it as though someone was listening—can help you see weaknesses in your story.

PART THREE: ENGAGING WITH READERS AND CREATING TRUE FANS

41

SURVEY SAYS...

How do you keep your fingers on the pulse of what interests your readers most? Try creating a short survey using jotform.com or surveymonkey.com (both free). Ask your readers to weigh in on new writing projects that you're considering.

Not sure where to take your book series next? Ask readers to vote on the next concept. Don't reveal everything, but this is a good way to gather ideas when you're trying to decide on a new direction.

For example, ask: Should Stella (the main character in your book)

A) find romance,

B) get a new job, or

C) go on an exciting new trip?

Allow room for readers to submit free-form comments because you may find interesting new ideas.

42
HANG OUT

Who are your readers? What do they like to do for fun? What do they buy? What do they do on weekends?

Are you one of them? Do you read other books in your genre? If not, you should.

Then, find out where readers who like the same books hang out online. Go to a meetup in your city.

Enjoy sci-fi and comics? Attend a comic book expo. They take place in many cities in the U.S. and Europe.

There's something out there for everyone. Find the authors you enjoy reading and sign up for their email lists. Reach out to them to say hello and that you enjoyed reading their books. Leave a glowing review for them.

If you enjoy shows such as *Game of Thrones* or *Westworld*, look for Facebook groups or websites such as quora.com where other fans hang out and discuss the series.

Be an observer and use the group for getting ideas. Don't go in with the intent of selling your books. Put in the time to develop relationships. Later, this may turn into sales.

To find true fans, you have to think like one.

43

SAY THANKS

In today's digital age, there is a sure way to get a smile. Send a handwritten thank-you card or letter. There are so many reasons to do this. Perhaps you guest-blogged for another writer or were interviewed on a podcast. Why not follow up with a handwritten note to show your gratitude?

How about sending thank-you cards to advanced copy readers who reviewed your book and left reviews?

Score bonus points for sending a signed copy of your book along with your thank-you note. Many people will follow up and post your note on social media, which goes even further to show that you took an extra step of kindness.

44

HOW TO HANDLE LOUSY REVIEWS

Every author's heart sinks when we receive negative reviews. No matter who you are, whether a debut author or a Pulitzer winner, there are always going to be people who don't like your work. Such is life.

Many new authors get upset when they receive a one- or two-star review on Amazon. The good news is that if you're getting a variety of ratings, people are reading your book.

I read the bad reviews and try to understand where the reader is coming from. Is this feedback I can learn from to improve my writing?

Sometimes the review doesn't provide any tangible information, and I typically ignore those. But often, you can discover some nugget of information. If you see a trend with people pointing out the same issues, then you should pay attention and fix whatever is wrong.

45

CO-WRITE WITH OTHER AUTHORS

Co-writing a book with another author has several benefits:

1. You produce another product faster than if you were both writing at the same time.
2. Both artists benefit from exposure to each others' audience.
3. As a bonus, you may pick up a few tips from another author and learn more about your own writing style.

When co-writing, put a simple contract agreement in place. This legal document determines who will be responsible for publishing and administering royalty payments, and defines what happens should anyone want to license the book.

46
BE AN EXHIBITIONIST

Show off your writing at events.

What conferences do your readers attend? Always seek potential new marketing opportunities. Entertainment and book expos are gaining in popularity in many large cities.

Several large cities in the U.S. have annual comic conventions. There are also multiple conferences for fans of the *Walking Dead* television and graphic novel series.

Book conventions are popular with young adult readers, letting fans gather and meet their favorite authors.

Have you attended any conferences? You may be surprised to find the cost of exhibiting your books is not as high as you thought. If you're on a limited budget, look into volunteering as a way to get into a conference and talk to fans.

47

THE LIBRARY IS YOUR FRIEND

Ever thought about getting your book into libraries?

Consider checking out libraries in your city. If possible, go during weekday daytime hours when you're likely to find a manager with decision-making power. Ask whether they offer books from local authors. Bring a few copies to leave in case they say yes or want to see your work. Don't show up a with a giant box of books as this would appear obnoxious!

Find out whether they have a program that showcases local authors, or know of literature events in the area. Libraries are a great source for finding community information.

Finally, be sure to patronize the library system. Become a member and get acquainted with their website, programs, and staff. This is a relationship that takes time to build but will be worth it in the end.

48

DON'T FORGET INDIE BOOKSTORES

Getting your book into stores is tough without a traditional publishing deal. The big chains won't help much; consider local independent bookstores instead. Chances are they may be looking for new content.

Start by checking out their websites to see if they have information for authors or list their staff members. Follow this up with a visit where you ask about including your book in their catalog.

Along with a few copies, bring a one-page description of your book that includes your sales blurb, author bio, and other positive info about your book (e.g., reader comments, editorial reviews, awards, etc.).

If you have impressive sales figures, be sure to mention this in your write-up. Bookstore owners want to know your book will sell, and showing social proof goes a long way.

Should the answer be no, politely thank the store manager, and follow up with an email or handwritten thank-you note expressing your gratitude for listening and how much you enjoy the store.

Be gracious and show goodwill. You never know—they might remember you and call you for their next author event.

49
IT'S ALL WHO YOU KNOW

One way to build your email subscriber list and find new readers is to collaborate with other authors in your genre. Here are a few ideas:

1. Approach another author and offer to give away one of your books for free to his or her readers. Ask the readers to opt-in to your email list in exchange for the free book.
2. Compile a bundle of free books between you and several authors. If you are the one putting this together, collect the email addresses for your list.
3. Co-host a webinar and provide free information to another author's readers. If you are promoting a training course as part of the webinar, make it a soft sell at the very end. Offer free and practical information first, then ask for permission to sell by asking the audience to stay on if they want to hear about your course/product.

Be sure to consider what value you are adding to the author's readers. That's the key to avoiding coming across as pushy.

50
REIGN IN YOUR SOCIAL MEDIA

How much thought have you given your social media profiles? Your picture and the blurb that describes who you are in a few characters is one of the first things new readers will see about you. Make sure your profile is the best it can be.

First, add a button to subscribe to your email list on your Facebook author page. Make this is a call-to-action button that appears along with the background photo on your page.

Many online businesses feature a "Shop Now" button, but you can instead feature a "Join Now" button and add text to your Facebook cover that makes it clear there is a free giveaway for signing up.

This approach is easy to set up once and works automatically in the background to gain you subscribers.

Second, update your social media profiles (or bio) with a link and text describing your free giveaway (e.g., Get my book, *50 Wonderful Writing Habits,* for FREE).

Platforms such as Twitter and Instagram have character limits for the bio section, so shorten your link using bitly.com or prettylinks.com.

Above all, be consistent. Use a professional head shot across your social media accounts so that you are recognizable.

51

CREATE A QUICK AND EASY EMAIL COURSE

Have you ever subscribed to a multi-day email program? These are ideal for authors because they don't require a lot of setup and they can be enticing for new email list subscribers.

This is a great stepping stone if you're considering creating a full-blown online course. Depending on your content, you could offer something simple like "10 Days to a Happier You."

Share your writing knowledge with the world by providing a daily writing tip for 30 days. Write your content in advance and then set up an autoresponder series using your email service. When readers opt-in, they'll automatically receive the emails.

Set it up once and forget it. Efficient!

52

LET YOUR WRITING SHINE ON WATTPAD

Wattpad.com lets authors publish their books for free and find new readers. Users on Wattpad publish stories, fan fiction, and poems, and vote and comment on stories.

You won't be able to sell your stories on Wattpad, but you can find new readers there. In 2014, the site had 35 million unique visitors per month. Many of the readers are younger, so Wattpad is perfect for YA authors.

To get started, set up a Wattpad account. As with Amazon, a good cover design will help get more eyes on your book. Study the works that are popular to see what readers are saying they like and don't like, then tailor your story accordingly. The Wattpad platform is an excellent way to experiment.

53

WHEN FICTION BECOMES (AUGMENTED) REALITY

Augmented reality is a future trend that's going to drive the growth of experience-driven content. Who could have predicted the phenomenal success of Pokemon Go, where players take part in an augmented reality using their smartphones? Apple and other retailers are looking at this new technology closely.

Writers and entrepreneurs have an opportunity. Consider how you could weave together reality with your fictional world. Or, imagine delivering a training course where you assign points for completing assignments in the real world.

The possibilities to engage with your audience are limitless.

54

WHAT WOULD ONLY A NATIVE KNOW?

Let's say you're writing a techno-thriller set in Paris. What is something only a local would know?

Research books and online to find a few nuggets of information that will surprise your readers. Work the elements into your story in a subtle way.

There are many excellent travel blogs that will give you insider tips and information about the cities and locations you want to learn about.

Better yet, network with other writers on social media to find someone who knows the city or country. I've answered questions such as, "What would be the best downtown Chicago bar for a thriller novel that has character and is not touristy?"

Answer: Ceres Café located in the Chicago Stock Exchange Building. According to a Yelp reviewer (a great tool to research establishments), you can "rub shoulders with trader-types in their smocks as well as fund managers closing their next big deal over a cocktail." Sounds like an interesting spot for some thriller action, wouldn't you say?

55

LISTEN TO THE EXPERTS

Are you writing a police procedural or crime thriller? Ask your network to recommend a real-life police officer or detective. A quick coffee or phone call can make a difference in getting accurate details into your story.

This is especially important if your main character has a rare occupation, such as a zoologist, vulcanologist, or trapeze artist.

Also consider asking your expert(s) to beta read your book to check details.

56

GROW YOUR READER LIST FASTER THAN A CHIA PET

Standing out in a crowded book marketplace is getting tougher. Consider what you are offering in exchange for people signing up for your email list. Unfortunately, it's not enough to say, "Sign up to receive my newsletter with weekly updates."

Readers are looking for value. Consider providing a free ebook as a giveaway. While you'll lose some sales, you'll gain email subscribers with whom you can start to build relationships. Over time, emails help grow your business. When trust is established, you may later sell books and other products.

Ideas to grow your list:

- Host a free webinar and make signing up for your email list a requirement to attend.
- Offer the webinar as a recording and make opting-in a requirement to download or access the webinar.
- Add a call to action at the end of emails, YouTube videos, blog postings, and any other shareable

content you generate (i.e., "To get a free ebook, click here").
- Include a subscriber testimonial next to your opt-in form.
- Hold a contest and make signing up for your email part of the entry requirements.
- Don't hide your opt-in form on your website. Make it prominent. Have your free giveaway be the first thing someone notices on your website.
- Nicely ask your social media followers to join.
- Include your free giveaway on your outgoing email signatures.

Your email list is one of your most valuable business assets. Nurture your readers and establish trust, and they will reward you in the long run.

57
TITLE THIS!

Start a contest for your readers. Ask them to come up with the title for your next book. Offer an exciting prize for the winner. Maybe the winner gets all your books for free forever, or the latest electronic gadget.

When you reach the top three finalists, conduct a survey of your readers and go out on social media to narrow down the winning title.

You never know what fascinating new ideas someone else will dream up!

58

THE SECRET OF MY SUCCESS

I'm not talking about the 1987 film starring Michael J. Fox despite it being great for 1980s nostalgia.

We all need good news these days. Why not share the successes that you've achieved on your blog, across social media, or in your newsletter?

What lessons did you learn that others could benefit from? What would you have done differently?

Perhaps your success story will encourage other writers. Pay it forward, and you'll be surprised at the help that comes back to you.

59
YES, AND...

There's a technique widely used in comedy improvisation troupes where the players are taught to always follow up another improv partner's idea with "Yes, and..."

They are coached never to answer in the negative because that could cut off an idea (and be awkward). All ideas are valuable and can lead the comedy sketch in many different directions.

Try applying this to writing in a few ways. First, what if you developed a character that always had a spirit of "Yes, and...?"

We're often approached with ideas from other writers or fans that at first cause us to scratch our heads. Instead of giving an immediate "No" answer, try "Yes, and..."

Consider the invitation with an open mind.

P.S. This is a great trick to use in arguments and when trying to influence people.

PERSUASION PRINCIPLES

Simple persuasive strategies help you engage with readers. Persuasion is not manipulation. Rather, it's getting people to do something that is in their best interest and that may also benefit you.

By learning a few persuasion principles, you can help convince readers to buy your books, keep reading to the end, or leave a review.

Basic concepts:

1. You have to be interested to be persuaded. We are most interested in ourselves, and spend much of our time thinking about love, money, or health. There is an art to consistently talking to people about them.
2. Reciprocity. The basic "this for that" concept is hard-wired into humans. When you provide a few small gestures, you can later ask for something in return. Think free books and other value you can offer your readers for free.
3. Persistence. The authors who keep asking for what

they want—and delivering value—will achieve results over time.
4. Create scarcity. When others desire something, we feel more compelled to want to buy it. We have a fear of missing out. Use this tactic for your business by offering a limited-time sale or a limited quantity.

PART FOUR: MARKETING TO SELL MORE BOOKS

61

THE BREAKFAST CLUB

You know your main character inside and out. You've lovingly crafted her intentions, driving motivation, and transformational arc.

You know what she ate for breakfast this morning.

The problem is, you're a little bored of her.

How can you add some personality and humor? Imagine her when she was in high school. Was she awkward, or one of the cool kids? What was her most embarrassing moment? Who was her favorite teacher? Did an incident occur that impacted the rest of her life?

Write a short story based on this and offer it as a free download when readers sign up on your website.

62

LESSONS LEARNED—OWN IT!

When we're in the middle of marketing and promoting our books, things are full-on crazy. It's a wonder we don't lose our minds. Have you considered writing down a list of what's working and what's a waste of your hard-earned cash?

I see many authors post to book advertising Facebook groups. I'm not saying it's the wrong choice, but I often wonder whether people are actually buying the books. Are you promoting your book to a group where your readers are hanging out?

Track your ads to see which ones are providing a return. This sounds boring until you start to realize that you can save a lot of money, not to mention precious time—time you could be spending writing more books.

Consider narrowing your advertising to one or two places. Amazon ads are terrific to focus on because that's where readers are buying books. Successful authors also use Facebook ads, Bookbub, and Freebooksy/Bargainbooksy. Those are great places to start. Try them for four weeks and write down what you learned.

63
GIMME, GIMME SOME GIVEAWAYS

Readers are not only looking for entertainment—they also love a good deal! Can you offer something unique that will stand out and make readers remember you?

Forget bookmarks (overdone). What will really stand out? Maybe it's a contest where you fly to the winner's home town and have dinner or drinks with them.

If you're artistic, design a t-shirt for five lucky winners. If you're a lousy artist like I am, commission a design on fiverr.com or 99designs.com.

The more personalized you make the giveaway, the better. Generate excitement by emailing your readers. Ask them to share on social media (and give them more chances to win the more they share).

THE PULP FICTION SECRET

I discovered an innovative way to hook readers. It's a powerful writing technique that was used in the 1994 film *Pulp Fiction*.

Closed-loop marketing is a concept that engages readers by introducing something compelling that the audience holds in their short-term memory. Thus begins an open loop, causing the audience to want to see a resolution. Then the content shifts to other matters, creating psychological tension because the audience wants to know the answer to the opening.

Remember the opening scene in *Pulp Fiction*? A couple sits at a diner, and we know them only by their pet names: Honey Bunny and Pumpkin. We soon learn they are criminals and decide to move from robbing liquor stores to robbing restaurants. Pumpkin stands on the table and announces "Everyone be cool, this is a robbery," and Honey Bunny yells her trademark line.

The movie credits roll and new scenes unfold.

Scene after scene, we don't see the diner again. The audience is wondering what happened. The movie is almost over before the end brings the diner robbery together with the other main characters played by Samuel L. Jackson and John Travolta. We find out that Honey Bunny and Pumpkin definitely chose the wrong diner to rob. The loop is closed, and we receive the answer to the question.

Another good example is the first book in George RR Martin's *A Song of Ice and Fire* series. In his first in the series, *A Game of Thrones*, we start out in a snowy forest with several members of the Nights Watchmen running into trouble. There are hints of mysterious creatures that live beyond the Wall, but Martin doesn't write about it again until much later in the series. The reader is left wondering what happened to them for a long time.

Use this same opening technique in your stories, on landing pages, in newsletters, and in blogs. Hook your reader early and share more story before you resolve the scenario.

Credit to Brian Clark's Unemployable podcast episode that explains the *Pulp Fiction* technique for creating engaging and compelling content. Check out his excellent podcast and writing on unemployable.com.

65
THE HOLY GRAIL OF BOOK ADVERTISING

Many indie authors consider a BookBub ad to be the holy grail of book marketing. The reason? Having your book selected for a BookBub "Featured Deal" reaches a large number of followers, and people are eager to gobble up books at low prices.

Bookbub is selective. According to a company representative, Bookbub receives 200 to 300 submissions per day, and only 10% to 20% of books get featured.

When you apply, be sure your cover and sales description are top-notch. When promoting a series, consider discounting the first book in series. Bookbub reports that doing so results in five times more sales for other books in your series.

Choose the lowest price point possible. Sales are 75% higher for books priced at $0.99. More established authors can run ads for books at $1.99 and $2.99, but newer writers should stick to $0.99.

Lastly, use links in your back matter. Bookbub shared that including links to your other books results in twice the sales of other books in the series.

Good luck!

66

MERCHANDISE YOUR BOOK

Are your readers clamoring for more? Consider offering merchandise that represents your writing. For fiction, this could be t-shirts with one or more characters and a signature quote.

Or you could commission an artist to create a coloring book for your fictional world.

For non-fiction writers, you could create a hardcover journal with quotes from your work. Other ideas may include coffee mugs, pens, and postcards.

Sell the merchandise from your website and bring some with you to speaking engagements. Small tokens will make you memorable to fans.

67

IF YOU BUILD IT, THEY WILL COME

If you're having a bad day, here's something to get excited about: The future looks good for writers.

Another three billion people will get smartphones by 2020.

Today, roughly 2.6 billion people have smartphones globally. That's over a third of the world's population. What's crazy is that by 2020, experts predict there will be 6.1 billion smartphones in circulation. The growth is led by a massive uptake in developing countries.

Often, I hear authors/entrepreneurs say, "I'm too late to market." No way! The data shows that there will be more readers and consumers of content. Start building your digital assets now and gain a foothold so that you can take advantage of the coming wave.

68

EMBRACE ARTIFICIAL INTELLIGENCE

Artificial Intelligence (AI) will change the way we interact. Machines are learning to read and understand human emotion better than ever.

What does that mean for us? Imagine that a blind person could wear computer-aided glasses that recognize faces and interpret a person's mood by observing body tone. What a life-changing difference that could make for so many people!

Let's take it further and imagine more possibilities. What if AI could be added to e-reader devices so that an author could receive data about how the reader's emotions change while reading their book? An author could learn which passages cause a spike in emotion or fear, or which scenes are boring.

Amazon shares data about books that are actually being read most frequently via amazon.com/charts.

I'm also excited about the rise of AI personal assistants. Google Assistant allows us to find help and automate online research. Amazon Echo was the top-selling new technology device in the 2016 holiday season. Expect Apple and Google to step up with similar products.

69

THE GOLDEN AGE OF TELEVISION

There is more and more amazing television content being created every day. Television viewing has changed significantly in the last few years due to streaming technology. We're no longer dependent on a few major broadcast channels. Companies like Amazon, Netflix, and HBO are creating content.

Game of Thrones and *Westworld* both compete with large-scale movie productions in terms of quality. The creators of the breakout hit show *Stranger Things* were rejected many times by traditional producers until Netflix decided to take a chance.

The good news for writers is there is a continued demand for quality content. Streaming content allows for a wide variety of genres that go narrow into a sub-niche. There's no more need to appeal to a mainstream audience. Exciting times!

What would you write for a 10-episode television show? Plot out each episode as you would plot a novel. Can you write a novella for each episode and release them one by one?

Later on, bundle your episodic novellas into one box set so that you have another creative asset.

70

MARKET LIKE A PRO

You're in this for the long haul. You want a career as a writer, and so you need to handle your marketing like a pro.

That means you need to understand your marketing inside and out. Maintain and constantly update a marketing list that has the following categories:

1. **Sales** - This is your key metric. Track the sales of your ebooks, print books, audio books, etc.
2. **Advertising channels** - Record the spend on any ads you run on Amazon, Google, Facebook, etc. Be sure to include the dates for each campaign, sales results, and return on investment.
3. **Social media** - Track any ads or page boosts you run. Consider also tracking your time on social media. Are your efforts leading to more sales or new email subscribers?
4. **Other marketing efforts** - Include any speaking events or conferences you attend. Are they leading to book sales?

Just like a company would, stop any marketing efforts that aren't yielding results.

71

CREATING CONTENT AT AN ELITE LEVEL

One key to success for writers is to produce consistently. Whether you write books, blogs, or screenplays, planning your production schedule can make a huge difference in your productivity, and ultimately your success.

Authors who operate at an elite level plan their content weeks, even months, in advance. Be like them.

There is power in writing down your plans. Create something as simple as a Google doc and list out what you are producing each month. Use a paper calendar if you prefer. Record your ideas about books you plan to release, blog topics, and any conferences where you are attending or speaking.

Over time, you'll appreciate how organized this will make you. When new ideas come up, or you get requests from others, always refer to your calendar to check your availability.

72

EARN INCOME WHILE YOU SLEEP

Unless you're Stephen King or J.K. Rowling, it's challenging to earn enough revenue from books alone to make a living. A simple way to supplement your income is to become an affiliate. You make money on sales of your books just by sending people to a unique affiliate link.

Sign up and become an affiliate with numerous affiliate programs. Hint: Amazon has a program that lets you earn a percentage of the sale of any products purchased within 24 hours after clicking on your affiliate link.

If you enjoy using certain products, try contacting the company to see if they offer an affiliate program. Often, they have an affiliate program because it helps them generate more sales.

Be patient. What starts out small—just a dollar or two a month—can add up over time and become hundreds of dollars a month for no work other than using specific links on your website and in your online advertising.

Don't miss out on this revenue-creating potential.

WHERE THE BUYERS ARE – AMAZON ADS

Many indie authors make most of their money selling books on Amazon. It's the largest market of online readers in the U.S. and other countries such as the U.K.

Knowing this, it makes sense to run ads for your book where you'll find your readers—on Amazon. The company offers an interface for setting up an ad campaign easily. Unlike Facebook, where you need to design an ad, the Amazon tool uses your book cover as the ad and lets you write a short blurb to sell your book.

First, sign up for the program by searching for Amazon Marketing Services, then set up your ad using the sponsored ad feature. You can also launch ads on a specific book from within your Kindle Direct Publishing (KDP) bookshelf.

Decide the daily budget that you want to spend ($5-$7) and bid on the CPC (cost per click), starting with $.08 to $.10. You're charged only when people click on your ad. Many authors find that the return on investment for Amazon ads is positive.

Select your own keywords (not the Amazon recommended ones) and start with at least 100 keywords for your first ad. Let the campaign run for at least a week because the sales data takes several days to catch up. Continue adding keywords so that you start building up to several hundred (even 1,000) keywords for maximum results.

74
SPY ON YOUR READERS

Ever wonder what your readers are buying online? What do they buy after purchasing your book? There are a few ways you can "spy" on your readers' consumer habits.

First, when you look up your book, you'll see a row towards the bottom that says "Customers who bought this item also bought." Scroll right or left, and you'll see many books listed.

Generally, you want your readers to be buying books that are similar to yours. This means your book is reaching the right audience. If you see many different types of books in your "Also Bought" area, it's time to rethink your book marketing.

Second, there's a nifty tool called Yasiv.com. Type in the name of a book, and it will show you a graphical map linking your book to customer book purchases. Filter to see what other non-book products were purchased if you're looking for affiliate product ideas.

How can you use this data? If you see that your readers are buying lots of books by a particular author, you can target the author's name as a keyword in either Amazon or Facebook ads to try to find more readers.

75
DEAR DIARY

A journal is an excellent product for your writer portfolio. Journals are simple to create. You can use motivational quotes or excerpts from your book. Try to reuse existing content rather than creating something new.

Add lines for people to write down their thoughts. Then, use Createspace.com to set up a print-on-demand paperback.

Be sure to order a proof copy (less than regular purchase price) and review it page by page to ensure your journal turned out as expected.

Journals also make great, customized gifts for friends and family. How cool would it be to get a journal designed by someone they know?

76

WINNING. EVERYONE LOVES A CONTEST

There's a lot of advice out there about the "right way" to run a book launch. The truth is there's no one way. Every book is different. What works for a big-name author with a publishing deal may not work for your dad who wants to self-publish a book about fly fishing.

A lot of authors stress about their book launches and agonize over little details. My advice is to try and have fun with it. If you do things right, you should have many book launches over a long career.

It's not about one book or one launch.

Try experimenting with your launches. I ran an experiment with a recent book launch where I ran a contest for my readers. When they bought my book, they received five free books of mine and were entered to win a prize—an Echo Dot.

I had a lot of success with this approach. It was my most successful launch ever. A few people told me I shouldn't handle my launch this way, but I trusted my instincts and went with it.

Of course, you need to have established a base of readers

or newsletter subscribers for this to work. And I probably wouldn't give away five books next time. Two or three bonus books is likely to be enough. More than that may overwhelm people, and the point is that you want them to read your new book.

Try it, experiment, and have fun.

77
GO WIDE

When it comes to ebook readership, Amazon has the largest market share. Therefore, most authors rely primarily on Amazon when it comes to book sales and marketing. So do I.

However, it's worth considering going broad and making your books available with other online book retailers.

Why? It's never good to rely on one company for your income. What would happen if Jeff Bezos suddenly woke up tomorrow and announced they were shutting down the ebook business?

While that scenario sounds unlikely, Amazon can and does change the rules—often. They drastically reduced the Kindle Unlimited income for authors. Remember, Amazon does what's in the best interest of its shareholders. Authors are just a tiny subset of customers.

So, how do you go wide? A simple way is to use Draft2Digital.com (D2D). You can distribute your books to many retailers at once, including Apple (iBooks), Kobo, and Barnes & Noble. There are also several non-U.S. retailers that get your book to new readers in other countries, such as Germany and Spain. D2D takes a small percentage of your sales price, but it's reasonable compared to having to sign up and load your book to each individual retailer.

Why not have your book available through other channels? As long as your book is not on Kindle Unlimited (where you **must** be exclusive to Amazon for 90 days), you can publish through other retailers.

In my experience, the KU exclusivity is helpful for your initial launch, but then it's better to go wide after that. I don't earn enough from KU to justify keeping my books exclusive.

78

GET OUT OF THE WRITER'S CAVE

It takes a village to raise a family, and the same can be said of an author's career. As much as our introverted selves want to sit at a desk and write and never talk to others, we can't prosper in isolation.

We need to share in the experience of other authors who have been there. And we need to give back to other aspiring writers who are just starting their journey.

Start making a list of people. Include other authors you already know, and those you want to know. Start reaching out slowly at first. Follow them on Twitter or Facebook. Comment on their blogs. Sign up for a course if they offer one. Thank them if you love their book.

Always offer value when you write someone. Don't ask for something until you've established a relationship. If you contact an author or celebrity asking for a book endorsement, provide several examples. Make it easy for them to respond and pick one.

Add to your list every week. Note the interaction and the date. Work at growing your network just like you work at writing and marketing your books. You'll be amazed at how quickly your network can grow, and how strong it will become over time.

79

IF WE TOOK A HOLIDAY...

When planning your book production schedule, consider launching new books around specific holidays. The time between Thanksgiving and New Year's Day is an excellent time to launch a new book. Many people are looking for gifts, receive new reading devices for the first time, and are also looking for books to read on holiday vacation.

You don't necessarily have to have a new book to launch. You can plan a new advertising campaign for an existing book or series if it makes sense for a holiday.

For example, I set up an ad campaign that focused on Groundhog Day to promote one of my existing books.

Other ideas:

- Valentine's Day - Romance or dating books
- Halloween - Horror or paranormal books
- Mother's Day - Mystery or self-help (health, wellness, aging)
- Father's Day - Crime and thrillers
- Easter - Christian books

80
PODCAST-A-PALOOZA

There are many excellent podcasts for authors, where you'll find incredible ideas for writing and marketing your books. I recommend:

- The Creative Penn Podcast (Joanna Penn)
- The Sell More Books Show (Jim Kukral and Bryan Cohen)
- Book Launch Show (Tim Grahl)
- Story Grid Podcast (Shawn Coyne and Tim Grahl)
- Science Fiction and Fantasy Marketing (Lindsay Buroka, Joseph Lallo, and Jeffrey M. Poole)
- Self-Publishing Formula Podcast (Mark Dawson)

PART FIVE: POSITIVE MINDSET AND TAKING CARE OF YOURSELF

81
JUST SAY NO

We writers want desperately to please our readers. We aim to delight, entertain, and educate. Not only that, we want to be responsive when fans write us or leave comments on our websites.

Add to this everything on our to-do list, and last but not least, we need to find the time to create every day.

Can you think of three things to which you can say "No?" How about removing three things from your to-do list? Things that, if they don't get done, the world won't end?

THE WALL OF SHAME

Let's face it: Getting bad reviews sucks. But it's inevitable. Every successful author, from J.K. Rowling to Harper Lee, has had some amount of lousy one- or two-star reviews.

The more you fight this, the more frustrated you'll become. As hard as it is, we must not waste our precious energy worrying about bad reviews. Despite begging and saying pretty please, Amazon won't remove negative reviews unless they are malicious.

Even though it's a beat down, you can rise above it through a positive mindset. Pick a theme song that shows you are better than your worst reviews. Here are a few ideas:

"Creep" by Radiohead

"Eye of the Tiger" by Survivor

"I Will Survive" by Gloria Gaynor

If your skin is tough enough, create a wall of shame where you pin the very worst reviews to a dart board. When you're having a bad day, turn up the volume on your song and let those darts fly.

A punching bag works well too. Show those reviewers you are the boss!

83
GO ON A WRITER'S RETREAT

Consider attending a writing retreat. Many organizations produce weekend or week-long trips designed for writers. Search "writer's retreat" online, and you'll find many ideas. Retreats range from the luxurious (Hawaii, Florida, and Mexico) to the rustic.

Don't like the idea of group situations? Consider creating your own writing retreat. A weekend retreat could be as close as taking a short road trip and finding an Airbnb cabin in the woods.

Regardless of where you go, be present in the moment. Bring your notebook everywhere to capture thoughts and observations. Don't put too much pressure on yourself to hit a certain word count. The retreat could be what you need to cultivate new ideas.

DITCH NEGATIVE SELF-TALK

Banish negative self-talk from your life. On a piece of paper, write down the bad advice your inner critic is giving you:

"I'm no good."

"I'm a failure."

"Everyone will hate my writing."

"I'll never be as good as _____."

"I'll never write again or have another idea."

Then ball it up and throw it in the trash. Do this as many times as you need to when you are battling negative self-talk.

85
BE THE RISING TIDE

"A rising tide lifts all boats" is an aphorism commonly used in economics. The better some do, the better off we all are.

We all know writers who are ahead of us and behind us. How often have other writers helped you learn new concepts, showed you new tools, or critiqued book covers and titles?

My hope is that you are generous with your help and support, too. When another writer asks for help, how do you respond?

Be known for your generosity and willingness to help. Karma will come back to you in good ways.

Start today.

86

THROW A BOOK FUNERAL

Ever given up on a book halfway through because it's just not working? We've all been there. It's no fun having to give up on a writing project, but sometimes it must be done.

Why not throw your book a funeral? Yes, I said it, and I meant it. When a book is just not working, give it a proper burial and pay your respects.

Invite a few writer friends who will understand and help support you. Deliver a short eulogy. Keep it light and fun. If anything, this can give you closure and help you move on to what's next.

87

TAKE A RIDICULOUS WRITER'S VACATION

Hemingway traveled to exotic places to write and spent time living in Spain, Cuba, and Key West. Could you go on a ridiculously amazing writer's trip?

There are many less-expensive travel opportunities these days. Set up a flight tracker on Google to be alerted when there are deals to your cities of choice. If you're able to travel on short notice, even better.

Airbnb and other home-share websites offer us the chance to live like a local rather than having to pay for expensive hotels. Likewise, ride-sharing apps have made it easy to get around.

Want to spend the summer writing in Thailand or Bali? Or maybe you want to spend April in Paris? With the right planning and a sense of adventure, you can make your travel dreams a reality.

88

THE WONDROUS WORLD OF IDEAS AROUND YOU

Ideas are everywhere, if you look for them.

I think a lot about writing every day, and how important practice is for those of us who want to make a living from writing. I say to myself, "Write every day no matter how many words. Just do it every day."

This means new words, not editing something you already wrote. Write new words every day, whether it's for books, a blog, your newsletter, or even your journal.

A lot of people ask me how this is possible. What if you run out of ideas, or don't have any?

Being open to ideas is about opening your mind. When you start writing, you develop your observation skills. Writers are often so introverted that we live inside our heads. The well of ideas within us can run dry if we aren't adding new sources of inspiration.

When you walk down the street, what do you think about? Are you living inside your head and recounting your to-do list, or reliving a past experience?

Next time, pay attention to your thoughts. Let them

move away from your internal monologue and quiet your mind so you experience the world around you.

89
TRUST EMERGENCE

Be open to new thoughts, experiences, and observations, and write them down. Carry a journal or use a device such as your phone to capture your notes.

Some people worry about how to organize these random thoughts. Should you add your notes to Evernote or another software tool?

What if you didn't worry about it, and kept the ideas in a notebook? Over time, the strongest ideas will emerge. Trust your subconscious to ruminate. The ideas that keep coming back to you are the ones to pursue.

90
REPEAT AFTER ME...

A lot of people think saying affirmations to yourself is a bunch of New Age garbage. To them, I ask, have you ever tried it?

Scott Adams, the creator of the *Dilbert* comic, wrote daily affirmations to himself, "I, Scott Adams, will be a famous cartoonist." He's written about multiple experiences in his life where the use of affirmations came true.

Is this magic?

Hardly. Affirmations help rewire our brains. Say something positive to yourself enough times, and you'll start to believe it. The same is true for people who are pessimistic. Ever notice how they seem to bring misfortune on themselves?

The brain is mysterious. When we repeat a statement to ourselves enough times, we subconsciously begin to not only believe, but to act.

Keep in mind that you must follow up your affirmations with action. It's not enough to repeat "I will be a famous author" and never put pen to paper. You must put the steps in place to achieve your goals, and the practice of saying or writing daily affirmations can help get you into the mindset where you will succeed.

Try it out. What have you got to lose?

91

HEALTH HACKS FOR YOUR WRITER'S BOD

Writers are sedentary. Studies show too much time spent sitting is harmful to our health. Plan to take a walk during your day, more if you can, and schedule the time in your calendar so you don't forget.

Another idea is to set a timer that goes off every hour. Let this be your reminder to get up and move. And I'm not talking about getting up to use the restroom or pour yourself another coffee. For three full minutes, push yourself to stretch, do walking lunges, and jump up and down. Three minutes at a time starts to add up over the course of a week.

Your body and your brain will thank you. Studies show physical activity helps us be more creative.

92

WHAT IS SUCCESS?

What is your definition of success? Do you want to win literary awards or sell enough books to quit your day job? What is the number you need to hit to have enough income?

Writing down a concrete definition of success means you have something to work toward. Absent a definition, you won't know what you're chasing after.

List your intellectual assets when you define success. If your plan is to write two books a year, list your assets each year for 5 years and 10 years into the future.

Make your definition tangible:

"In one year, I will have two published books."

"In 5 years, I will have 10 published books."

"In 10 years, I will have 20 published books."

Include how many of your books will be in digital, print, and audio. Having a variety of products means more sales and more income.

Then, define what success means on your terms. How many books do you need to sell each month to earn a living? Maybe you don't want to quit your job; instead, your books supplement your income.

Regardless of what you seek, know your goal so that you recognize it when you find it.

93

MEET FUTURE YOU

Knowing your definition of success is the first step. Next, envision your success at the level you want to achieve. Write a biography of future you, after you've achieved the success you seek.

> "Zoe P. Author is an award-winning author who has sold over 100,000 copies of her *Awesome Sauce Zombie* series. Her work has been translated into 18 languages.
>
> Zoe is an accomplished speaker and co-writes with other talented horror authors. She is pursuing a possible television series with Netflix."

Have fun with this. Dream big.

94
TOOT THAT HORN

Job search experts recommend maintaining a list of accomplishments that you can easily refer to during your next job interview. I recommend you do this for your writing.

Keep a running list any time you achieve one of your goals, such as publishing a new book or releasing your book in audio. Should you be interviewed on TV or a podcast, also add that to your brag list.

For an extra boost, hang your accomplishment list on your wall. You'll love how it grows over time.

Otherwise, you may forget all the little steps along the way to your greatness.

95
BUILD A TREADMILL DESK

A treadmill desk is an excellent way for writers to stay healthy and fit while they continue to write. There are inexpensive models of flat treadmill bases. Place one under an existing desk, purchase a stand-up desk riser, and you have a ready-to-go treadmill desk.

Start slowly and adjust to walking while you work. Over time, you will learn how to type when walking. And if you don't like that, learn to dictate as you walk.

Be sure to track your steps using a wearable device, and enjoy the progress you'll make walking as you write.

96

RIDE IN THE BACK OF A POLICE CAR

This is a test. Are you still reading?

If you've never ridden in a police car, that's good. What would you imagine it would be like? How about for someone new to the country who doesn't speak our language?

If you have been in the back of a cop car, why? Write about the experience. Would you have done anything differently? What if the officer who arrived on the scene was someone you knew?

P.S. Don't take this as advice to do something that will get you into a police car. :-)

97

ABANDON YOUR GUILT

Do you feel guilty sometimes when you write? Maybe there's a tiny voice in your head that says you might be a selfish person, or that you're self-absorbed.

Don't worry; this is common. I felt guilty when I quit my job to write full time. I wondered what I was doing when I spent much of a recent summer indoors writing.

Many of my non-writer friends didn't understand my new career choice. What they wrote off as a hobby became my full-time job, and that freaked some people out.

Some people wondered how it was possible for me to write for a living. Others wondered how they could change their careers to something they loved, too. I felt guilty for having the ability to do what I loved when many others didn't.

Ultimately, I realized life is too short to worry about what others think. We are all on this earth for a reason. We each choose how we use our time. That's the beauty of life.

I chose to write and create, and to stop feeling guilty about it.

What do you choose?

98
GIVE BACK

Volunteer in your community or at a non-profit organization to share your writing story. Perhaps you could encourage people who need help to journal or start writing their own personal stories.

Non-profits are often understaffed. They need you! Consider sharing your writing, editing, and marketing expertise with others.

Giving back and serving your community are excellent ways to get out of your head when you're stuck on a plot point, or when you are between novels.

We introverted authors need to get out sometimes!

99
SOAK IN THE SUDS

Being a writer means hours spent writing on a computer and sitting way too much. This often leads to sore muscles, especially when you're on a writing binge.

Try running a hot bath and pouring in a cup or two of Epsom salt. The salt breaks down into magnesium and sulfate, which help relax sore muscles and loosen stiff joints.

Try the bath once or twice a week to feel better and reduce stress. Who knows what ideas you may come up with while in the tub?

100

GET YOUR MOJO BACK

The writing life is sedentary, there's no doubt about that. Writing can also be an isolating experience where we stay indoors more often than not, and get wrapped up in our own heads.

There have been weeks when I didn't leave my house for four or five days at a time, when I was deep into a project or handling a book launch. I'm not proud of this, and I've confirmed this same pattern with other writer friends when they are up against deadlines.

Our connected world has also made it easier to talk to people less and less. We order our groceries, get meals delivered, and bank online now. It's common to travel around cities never talking to anyone because you have ear buds in.

We cannot stay inside our heads all the time. It's not healthy for us, and our writing will be the worse for it. Try to take time every day to walk outside, breathe in fresh air, and experience the world without feeling like you must be productive.

Think of it as a time to "get your mojo back." Maybe a

little distance from your day-to-day routine can help you see around an obstacle or solve a problem.

CONCLUSION

Thank you for joining me on this journey. You and I are in it together, my author friend. I can't imagine a life without writing. Can you?

I hope that you enjoyed your 100 two-minute digestible writer vitamins!

If you enjoyed this book, I would greatly appreciate an honest review. Contact me at info@projectmanagerwriter.com with any questions, or just drop a note to let me know what you thought of this book.

I would love to hear your awesome ideas for authors. What did I miss? Maybe your idea will land in the next version of this book.

Interested in free updates on writing and self-publishing, including news, tips, and free books? Please visit my website, ProjectManagerWriter.com.

Happy Writing,
Courtney Kenney

Want to become a more productive and prosperous author? Get a free eBook, *The Productive Author Roadmap*, at ProjectManagerWriter.com.

ABOUT THE AUTHOR

Courtney Kenney is an author and book launch consultant. She spent 16 years working as a project manager at technology companies. She left corporate nine-to-five life behind and now runs her own author business.

Courtney helps authorpreneurs launch bestselling books and grow their author platforms. She lives in Chicago with her husband and loves walking, exploring new neighborhoods, traveling, and playing in a skeeball league.

Visit her website, ProjectManagerWriter.com, where she writes about becoming a more productive and prosperous author.

———

More books by Courtney Kenney:

Creating Space to Thrive: Get Unstuck, Reboot Your Creativity and Change Your Life

Layoff Reboot: Bounce Back from Job Loss and Find a Career You Love

Unleash Your Author: Write a Book in 30 Days

7-Step Book Launch Plan: Strategies to Publish and Promote Your Book

———

Connect with Courtney online:

Instagram/authorunleashed

www.ProjectManagerWriter.com
info@projectmanagerwriter.com

Printed in Poland
by Amazon Fulfillment
Poland Sp. z o.o., Wrocław